Gypsy Rickwood's
Fortune - Telling Book

" From the truth to a lie is but a hands-breadth."—
Romany Proverb.

NEW YORK
E. P. DUTTON & CO. INC.

First printing - - - Feb., 1929
Second printing - - March, 1929
Third printing - - - March, 1929

Printing Statement:

Due to the very old age and scarcity of this book, many of the pages may be hard to read due to the blurring of the original text, possible missing pages, missing text and other issues beyond our control.

Because this is such an important and rare work, we believe it is best to reproduce this book regardless of its original condition.

Thank you for your understanding.

PREFACE

In offering this little book to the English-speaking public it is hoped that it may give good counsel to many and an hour of amusement to those who regard it simply as a game.

The method is a very old one, practised by wandering tribes of gypsies long before it was ever set down roughly on paper, and the answers to the questions have been slightly modernized by the translator. It may be emphasized, however, that the accuracy of the answers depends largely on the sincerity of the questioner. Thus, if questions of an unsuitable nature are asked, the answers will be in the same frivolous vein.

METHOD OF TELLING A FORTUNE

Take an ordinary deck of cards. All fifty-two cards, after being well shuffled, should be placed face down in the form of a horse-shoe on the table. Concentrate steadily and then draw a card. The number and suit on the card corresponds with the number of the answer to the question which has been asked.

This process should be repeated between each section in cases where all the questions are put.

INDEX OF QUESTIONS

INDEX OF QUESTIONS

Concerning Chance—Answers, pages 82-111.

INDEX OF QUESTIONS

CONCERNING LIFE

With a boyar's lie one goes round the whole of Hungary.
ROUMANIAN PROVERB.

AM I DESTINED FOR SUCCESS ?

Diamonds.

1. Certainly.   No one can take the Ace of Trumps.
2. Not by your own efforts.
3. Hectic and brief.
4. Yes, but not of the kind you expect.
5. Your hopes will be frustrated.
6. In every case a near relative will prevent it.
7. After many disappointments.
8. Yes, but not in the eyes of the world.
9. Your success will bring you much grief.
10. At the cost of your conscience.
Kn. Far better if you were not.
Qn. Through a woman's influence.
Kg. Yes, you have a friend at Court.

Hearts.

1. Yes, though you had best say very little about it.
2. You are pushed into it by an ambitious relative.
3. You have not enough energy.
4. You are too sensitive.
5. A social one.
6. Artistically—never.
7. You do not wish for it.
8. You will inherit it.   It runs in the family.
9. You will outdistance all competitors.
10. With your tongue, O, Artful one !
Kn. Because of your audacity.
Qn. A doubtful one.
Kg. In a canter.

AM I DESTINED FOR SUCCESS?

Clubs.

1. By reason of your persistence.
2. A rather unsatisfactory success.
3. You will be let down at the last minute.
4. Too much jealousy for you to succeed easily.
5. The sun will always shine upon you.
6. So great that the world will applaud it.
7. Your light-hearted carelessness will achieve it unceasingly.
8. Follow your star.
9. Yes.
10. The sea will bring it to you.
Kn. Without effort.
Qn. A limited one.
Kg. When in the early twenties.

Spades.

1. Yes, because you are so tenacious.
2. By crooked ways.
3. A literary one.
4. Through bluff.
5. You will be a popular Hero (or Heroine).
6. Through your children.
7. You are a born climber.
8. You will never do so.
9. By marriage.
10. Chance will assist you.
Kn. It is rather a forlorn hope.
Qn. You will receive public recognition.
Kg. A high title awaits you.

WHAT PROFESSION SHOULD I FOLLOW?

Diamonds.

1. You would succeed as a public speaker.
2. Try Emigration.
3. Latent dramatic ability indicated.
4. You are marked as a leader of men.
5. Avoid the profession of Medicine.
6. Don't go into the Church.
7. You would succeed as a dancing instructor.
8. Take yourself more seriously and you could do anything.
9. You are born to be a Poet.
10. Why not Fleet Street?
Kn. Alas, I see nothing before you but the life of a lounge-lizard.
Qn. Should advise Market Gardening.
Kg. Fame awaits you in a City office.

Hearts.

1. You are a dreamer, not a worker.
2. Anything connected with wheels.
3. As a producer.
4. You do not desire any profession.
5. Teaching the young idea.
6. Designing clothes.
7. The sea.
8. The Army.
9. Commerce.
10. Architecture.
Kn. Athletics.
Qn. Something connected with Commerce.
Kg. A sedentary occupation.

14

WHAT PROFESSION SHOULD I FOLLOW?

Clubs.

1. You are a gambler and will not work.
2. The Stage.
3. Woods and fields are your province.
4. Agriculture.
5. Sleight of hand.
6. Addressing a crowd.
7. That of an Agitator.
8. Travel for a profession.
9. Office work.
10. Shipping.
Kn. You will need none.
Qn. A Captain of Industry.
Kg. You will always be an amateur.

Spades.

1. A University job.
2. Politics.
3. Chemistry.
4. Anything but work.
5. Writing.
6. Real Estate.
7. A middleman.
8. Hotel keeping.
9. A Beachcomber.
10. The Civil Service.
Kn. The Law.
Qn. The retired life of a scholar.
Kg. A gossip writer of society paragraphs.

15

SHALL I BECOME NOTORIOUS ?

Diamonds.

1. The world will exclaim when your name is mentioned.
2. An unenviable notoriety.
3. For charitable works.
4. As a promoter of commercial projects.
5. As a collector.
6. For great absent-mindedness.
7. You will live and die in obscurity.
8. For consistent success at cards.
9. For your extreme tidiness.
10. For carrying your liquor like a gentleman.
Kn. For your dissipated habits.
Qn. Through refusing to pay your bills.
Kg. For the eccentricity of your clothes.

Hearts.

1. Too much for your liking.
2. You will be largely photographed.
3. For your excellent manners.
4. As a judge of wine.
5. As a celebrated talker.
6. As the Club Bore.
7. For your mystery.
8. As a gossip.
9. As a gourmand.
10. As a connoisseur.
Kn. For your powers of mimicry.
Qn. As a noted " character."
Kg. For your saintliness.

SHALL I BECOME NOTORIOUS?

Clubs.

1. For your racy conversation.
2. As a good—if dull—friend.
3. For the number of your love affairs.
4. For your laugh.
5. Your intrepidity will astound all.
6. For your cleverness in manipulating situations.
7. As a wise adviser.
8. In the bankruptcy courts.
9. Very much so, in the newspapers.
10. Only for a time, and that unpleasantly.
Kn. As a snob.
Qn. For your excellent taste.
Kg. As an artist.

Spades.

1. It is doubtful.
2. If you try hard enough.
3. Because you have kept your youth.
4. In argument.
5. As a political prophet.
6. For your extraordinary luck.
7. Because of your beard.
8. No. You are a nonentity.
9. For strength of character.
10. For general eccentricity.
Kn. Do not ask why.
Qn. For extravagance.
Kg. Because of your charm.

SHALL I BE GREATLY SOUGHT AFTER ?

Diamonds.

1. Yes; if you can overcome your bashfulness.
2. No, you will be avoided.
3. You are too masterful.
4. You will be pursued by your friends.
5. You are adored by the opposite sex.
6. Only when you cease to talk.
7. You are too melancholy.
8. A cynic is never popular.
9. You are too easily shocked.
10. Don't talk politics and a change for the better will soon come.
Kn. Don't talk golf and bridge and your friends will like you better.
Qn. Love animals and children and all will be well.
Kg. Not while you wear that hat.

Hearts.

1. By fits and starts.
2. By all manner of people.
3. While you are in your present position. Not later on.
4. If you adapt yourself better to circumstances.
5. For your art.
6. Because you impress on sight.
7. Not sincerely so, I fear.
8. While your luck holds.
9. Because of your cook.
10. Because people fear you.
Kn. For what you give so generously.
Qn. For your high spirits.   [mystery.
Kg. Yes, to discover your real occupation, which is a

SHALL I BE GREATLY SOUGHT AFTER?

Clubs.

1. You lay yourself out to be.
2. Cheerfulness does it.
3. Your unvarying hospitality causes it to be so.
4. If it were not for a near relative you would be.
5. Your heartlessness isolates you.
6. Yes, by strange people.
7. All your life.
8. To sit upon committees.
9. To fill up gaps.
10. Yes, because you repeat scandal.
Kn. For working parties.
Qn. As an oracle.
Kg. By borrowers.

Spades.

1. To get up concerts or shows.
2. To open bazaars.
3. For dances.
4. For useful but not entertaining events.
5. As a consoler.
6. You are wanted by the police.
7. When all else fails.
8. As a boon companion.
9. For foreign travel.
10. Socially.
Kn. Because of your wisdom.
Qn. To smooth things over.
Kg. As a peaceful element in any house.

SHALL I GO LONG VOYAGES ?

Diamonds.

1. You will never cross the sea.
2. Yes. You will cross the ocean and find fame.
3. There is danger to you by sea.
4. One long and one short voyage.
5. Many short voyages.
6. You will go once too often.
7. Once round the world.
8. To cold seas.
9. You are too bad a sailor. Try flying.
10. East or West home is best. Stay there.
Kn. Many Cook's Tours.
Qn. Yes, but always steerage.
Kg. Often and in the greatest luxury.

Hearts.

1. Yes.
2. When you least desire it.
3. You will see the palms and temples of the East.
4. To the snows.
5. With consistently bad weather.
6. You will live to wear a life-belt.
7. Yes, in a tramp steamer.
8. No.
9. Ultimately.
10. Quite suddenly.
Kn. On account of indisposition.
Qn. In your imagination.
Kg. On business.

SHALL I GO LONG VOYAGES ?

Clubs.

1. Better not.
2. Yours is the sign of the Blue Peter.
3. Always for pleasure.
4. Very unlikely.
5. One.
6. To meet your fate.
7. Across the Atlantic.
8. To southern seas.
9. Channel crossings.
10. Some long, some short.
Kn. Rough waters.
Qn. In curious company.
Kg. Favourable circumstances attend your journeys.

Spades.

1. You will do well to stay at home.
2. You wish to voyage and will do so.
3. Yes, professionally.
4. Until you tire of it.
5. As a cure for heart-break.
6. A honeymoon journey.
7. Never.
8. You will prefer dry land and not without cause.
9. Six times through the Bay of Biscay.
10. Yes, but you will be glad to return.
Kn. Summer seas always for you.
Qn. You will double the Cape like old sherry.
Kg. No.

WHY DO PEOPLE LOVE ME?

Diamonds.

1. Because of your smile.
2. They don't.
3. Because of your sense of humour.
4. You tell such good stories.
5. Because you flatter.
6. You are simply irresistible.
7. Because you are a dependable friend.
8. Your mental qualities overcome the plainness of your features.
9. Because of your eyes.
10. Your Bank balance answers this question.
Kn. Because of your success.
Qn. Because you are so good-looking.
Kg. Entirely due to Personal Magnetism.

Hearts.

1. They think you worth it.
2. All the world loves a lover.
3. They cannot help it.
4. Your naïveté.
5. Your ready answers.
6. The illusion you can create.
7. You are always optimistic.
8. Because you are so safe.
9. You represent Romance.
10. You have a way with you.
Kn. Your delightful voice.
Qn. You understand them.
Kg. You feed them so well.

WHY DO PEOPLE LOVE ME?

Clubs.

1. It is doubtful that they do.
2. Some do, others do not.
3. Because you are a Rake.
4. Your intense respectability is liked by some.
5. Your patience is the cause.
6. Their admiration is only skin-deep.
7. They do not know how faithless you are.
8. You make them laugh.
9. You have great power.
10. You can introduce them to the Lions.
Kn. Your wilfulness attracts.
Qn. They dare not appear not to.
Kg. There is no rift in your lute.

Spades.

1. They think you ill-used.
2. You can deal with them.
3. You are so good at games.
4. Because you baffle them.
5. You make them feel happy.
6. Your stern sense of duty.
7. Your charitable nature.
8. You lend everything you have and never ask for it back.
9. Because they do not know you.
10. Your frivolity.
Kn. That warm hand-shake.
Qn. Oh those eyes !
Kg. For yourself.

SHALL I LIVE AT HOME OR ABROAD ?

Diamonds.

1. You would make a splendid colonist.
2. Your country needs you.
3. Try to resist the lure of Monte Carlo.
4. Avoid the Continent.
5. A fruit farm in South Africa awaits you.
6. The lights of Hollywood blaze on your far horizon.
7. The provincial town is your native heath.
8. The East calls you.
9. The vast prairies are your home.
10. Live deep in the country and be content.
Kn. Try a manufacturing town in the coal district.
Qn. Avoid seaports.
Kg. Live on an island.

Hearts.

1. Try staying at home.
2. Your family will wish you to travel.
3. Your circumstances keep you in London.
4. Do not be so restless.
5. You will travel but not remain abroad.
6. Keep away from Paris—a bad place for you.
7. Your roots are in the British Isles.
8. In Caledonia stern and wild.
9. The Carpathians are your spiritual home.
10. The wide world is your play-ground.
Kn. Not far from the Uxbridge Road.
Qn. In theatre-land.
Kg. In a modern Babylon.

SHALL I LIVE AT HOME OR ABROAD ?

Clubs.

1. Never for long anywhere.
2. In a rose garden.
3. By a river.
4. Near great woods.
5. Five minutes from the church and railway [station.
6. In an ancient town.
7. A cathedral town.
8. An Indian bungalow.
9. On the Border.
10. Across the sea.
Kn. Always in hotels.
Qn. In the wettest country on earth.
Kg. Quietly in a London house.

Spades.

1. You should think well what you wish for, for you will get it.
2. A cottage by the sea.
3. In a very artistic quarter.
4. Surrounded by the noises of a farm yard.
5. Under the deodars.
6. Never go abroad.
7. On the wild moors will be best for you.
8. A caravan is best suited for your tastes.
9. You would feel at home in a suburb.
10. Try a complete change.
Kn. In a narrow street in Paris.
Qn. You prefer open spaces.
Kg. You are a wanderer.

WILL MY PRESENT PERPLEXITIES BE SOLVED?

Diamonds.

1. Never unless you change your tactics.
2. As soon as you give up your besetting sin.
3. Yes, through the agencies of a friend.
4. The storm is only gathering.
5. Your own conscience will best answer this.
6. A little consideration for others might help.
7. When you think less of your personal appearance.
8. In a year's time.
9. When the truth comes out.
10. Tell the truth and see what happens.
Kn. Be less arrogant and things will improve.
Qn. When you cease to borrow from your friends.
Kg. If you smoke less.

Hearts.

1. When you calm yourself.
2. They are at the mercy of the actions of others.
3. Satisfactorily.
4. Yes.
5. If you trust your friend. [sibility.
6. Not until you are prepared to undertake respon-
7. I doubt it.
8. Be less quarrelsome and they will.
9. Look on the bright side of things.
10. By a cheque.
Kn. Unexpectedly.
Qn. Only partially.
Kg. With great happiness.

WILL MY PRESENT PERPLEXITIES BE SOLVED ?

Clubs.

1. You will hear something which will help you.
2. Make no decision for a week.
3. It depends upon the good offices of another.
4. With startling dénouements.
5. Very satisfactorily.
6. Trust no one in this matter and all will be well.
7. An unexpected letter will assist you greatly.
8. Very soon.
9. They exist only in your imagination.
10. Give yourself no cause for regrets a year hence.
Kn. Follow the dictates of your conscience.
Qn. How is it possible ? Certainly not.
Kg. You are out of the wood.

Spades.

1. Fate will act.
2. Don't be in such a hurry.
3. As you yourself desire.
4. Yes, but by a total stranger to you.
5. The solution comes across water to you.
6. Try not to be so nervous about it.
7. Patience and they will.
8. Never in your present frame of mind.
9. Very simply. The person you are worried by will disappear.
10. A change of air will do it.
Kn. An Agony in the *Times* should help you.
Qn. You talk too much about them.
Kg. Watch for an unexpected message.

WILL MY LIFE BE ADVENTUROUS ?

Diamonds.

1. Only too much so. Beware !
2. By flood and field.
3. You will seek adventures and find them.
4. Chiefly through your own lack of caution.
5. Your life will be monotonous and quiet.
6. Your psychic tendencies will make it so.
7. One only, and that will change your fate.
8. In later years.
9. Adventures of a highly undesirable nature.
10. Yes, but all's well that ends well.
Kn. You spend your life looking for trouble.
Qn. Fill of change and dismay.
Kg. Cards and champagne will make it so.

Hearts.

1. If adventures do not happen, you will invent them.
2. Not without shocks.
3. No.
4. Curiously so.
5. The adventures of others will affect you.
6. Yes.
7. At times.
8. You cannot avoid a cataclysm.
9. The person you love most drags you into danger.
10. No, very peaceful and dull.
Kn. Full of variety.
Qn. In small ways.
Kg. Coloured with Romance.

28

WILL MY LIFE BE ADVENTUROUS?

Clubs.

1. To the end.
2. Monotonous.
3. There will be one great adventure.
4. Variable and interesting.
5. Not while you remain where you are.
6. No, always below high-water mark.
7. Be careful—one nears you now.
8. The shadow of a coming event lies across your path.
9. Next year.
10. Your adventures are all over.
Kn. You will be very reluctant to meet them.
Qn. Your daring spirit creates situations.
Kg. Always ending well.

Spades.

1. Look out for squalls.
2. Boredom will drive you into danger.
3. It has been, is, and will be.
4. Your well-wishers hope not.
5. Restrain your impulses and live quietly.
6. Humdrum.
7. Not specially so.
8. The attentions of the great will make it so.
9. This depends upon yourself.
10. Do try to settle down.
Kn. Doubt and deceit will make it so.
Qn. You will gamble with success.
Kg. Choose the middle path, it is safest.

SHALL I ATTAIN MY HEART'S DESIRE ?

Diamonds.

1. No.
2. When you are in Scotland in November.
3. Only by craft.
4. Fair and honest dealing will help.
5. By the accident of Fate.
6. Dark as it is, you will.
7. You change it too often.
8. When the lilacs bloom.
9. Yes, and regret that it is so.
10. No, you are too fickle.
Kn. You have not sufficient energy.
Qn. With your splendid character you are sure to.
Kg. Your personal charm will help you.

Hearts.

1. Yes, with more than ordinary luck.
2. Do you deserve to ?
3. The prospect is brightening.
4. After long years.
5. Sooner than you expect.
6. You will regret it when you do.
7. One person, known to you, prevents it.
8. You will change your aim.
9. At the last moment you will be disappointed.
10. When all seems lost, success arrives.
Kn. Try to limit your aspirations.
Qn. Concentrate more steadily and you may.
Kg. In six weeks' time.

SHALL I ATTAIN MY HEART'S DESIRE?

Clubs.

1. By a way you have not yet imagined.
2. Cease to brood over it and you may.
3. It would be very inadvisable if you did.
4. The odds are in your favour.
5. You are so heartless, how is it possible?
6. For a short time.
7. Yes, but you will have to wait.
8. Gloriously.
9. If you cease to make a fool of yourself.
10. In the near future.
Kn. With reservations.
Qn. Try to forget it.
Kg. It concerns too many people and is unlikely.

Spades.

1. A friend will help you.
2. Drop it like a hot potato.
3. It is completely unsuitable that you should.
4. Sweet are the uses of adversity. You will not.
5. Eventually.
6. Without an effort on your part.
7. It is the desire of the moth.
8. In reality it is only a will-o'-the-wisp.
9. When the Autumn comes.
10. You had far better not.
Kn. A trick will procure it.
Qn. You win it with your smile.
Kg. In the end.

HOW SHALL I RECOGNIZE MY ENEMY?

Diamonds.

1. Danger lies where you least expect it.
2. He comes regularly to your house.
3. Beware of a man with a limp.
4. You will meet him in a fortnight's time.
5. Under peculiar circumstances.
6. He is in a position of high authority.
7. A woman, fair and bitter of tongue.
8. To be found in the servants' hall.
9. Sits opposite to you at the card table.
10. Very musical.
Kn. Wears the face of a friend.
Qn. One under your authority.
Kg. You have no enemies.

Hearts.

1. Has travelled far and wide.
2. Small and very alert. Watch him well.
3. A gloomy face and a cold smile.
4. A sweet manner covers a venomous tongue.
5. Dark and sinister.
6. One who once loved you too well.
7. A business connection ties you together.
8. Means no harm but is too weak.
9. Sly eyes.
10. Wears the garb of piety.
Kn. So charming that she disarms you at every turn.
Qn. Through an old jealousy dating from childhood.
Kg. Means only to be friendly.

HOW SHALL I RECOGNIZE MY ENEMY?

Clubs.

1. One of those subtle, inexplicable jealousies accounts for it.
2. Has hated you long from a distance.
3. Your enemy is a politician.
4. One whom you have only just met.
5. Someone who reads other people's letters.
6. A secret foe, and one of your own household.
7. The man you injured.
8. He covers his dislike by great heartiness of manner.
9. A poor creature who is at your mercy.
10. A person you employ.
Kn. The woman you injured.
Qn. A secretive and silent personage.
Kg. Someone we all know.

Spades.

1. The person you helped last year.
2. A sycophant who fawns upon you.
3. A grim and honest enemy.
4. A very young person.
5. Invites you often to his house.
6. A merciless cynic who lampoons you.
7. A giggling, tittering woman.
8. Someone you know too much about.
9. A person who is only a casual acquaintance.
10. A powerful and unscrupulous man.
Kn. Your confidential servant.
Qn. Your legal adviser.
Kg. Your mother-in-law.

SHALL I BE RICH?

Diamonds.

1. Never.
2. By great luck.
3. Hard work will bring a sufficiency.
4. In the strangest way wealth will come.
5. You will inherit a large property.
6. A rich relative will leave you a fortune.
7. An act of kindness will bring you unexpected luck.
8. Your unscrupulous methods will land you in difficulties.
9. You will gamble once too often.
10. Take care, your position is perilous.
Kn. A modest competency.
Qn. Yes, but you will lose it.
Kg. You have too fine a nature to desire wealth.

Hearts.

1. Enormously so.
2. Yes.
3. By repute but not in fact.
4. It will be all spent educating your family.
5. Be careful how you invest your savings.
6. A fluctuating income.
7. Enough for one but no more.
8. You will always pull through.
9. Money melts in your hands.
10. When you get it you will not keep it.
Kn. You only want money to burn.
Qn. Yes, through a woman.
Kg. You are lucky in investments.

SHALL I BE RICH?

Clubs.

1. By honest toil.
2. You will win a celebrated sweepstake.
3. By a clever invention.
4. Your play will succeed.
5. Your long sycophancy will pay you moderately.
6. You have the Crœsus touch,
7. By dealing in Real Estate.
8. By inheritance.
9. You never will.
10. Not by backing winners.
Kn. You will strike oil.
Qn. Open a fresh door.
Kg. Try Pelmanism.

Spades.

1. You would succeed at inn-keeping.
2. Anything connected with the Arts will be successful.
3. You will live quietly on an invested capital.
4. Land will be lucky for you.
5. When you cross running water.
6. You are too generous ever to be wealthy.
7. You will inherit your fortune.
8. Riches will pour upon you.
9. You will succeed at everything you touch.
10. You will always be dependent on others.
Kn. A great future awaits you smiling.
Qn. You are one of the idle rich already.
Kg. You would have been far happier poor.

AM I WASTING MY TALENTS ?

Diamonds.

1. You have none.
2. Yes, your environment is wrong.
3. You are bound to succeed in anything.
4. You should seek a change.
5. Unfortunately you have no choice.
6. Be patient.
7. You will find your proper expression in time.
8. Do not despise small beginnings.
9. Nothing is ever wasted.
10. At least it is better than this time last year.
Kn. You are more appreciated than you suppose.
Qn. In the end you will win through.
Kg. In your case talent is lost in genius.

Hearts.

1. By no means.
2. Your talents are of the domestic order and are useful.
3. Yes, you ought to try something active.
4. You are afraid to trust yourself.
5. Frittering them away.
6. Lethargy prevents success.
7. Your temperament is against you.
8. You are a good plodder, go on.
9. You change too often.
10. You are afraid to embark on something new.
Kn. Yes, because you love a mediocre personality.
Qn. You are gifted greatly.
Kg. Family cares handicap you.

AM I WASTING MY TALENTS?

Clubs.

1. Your political activities absorb you too deeply.
2. You are intrigued against.
3. Make a fresh start.
4. Health will be your difficulty.
5. Your ambition bids you go on.
6. You are a born teacher of the young.
7. Concentrate more.
8. The interruptions of your life are a great hindrance.
9. You must be more content with small results.
10. See life through your own eyes, not those of others.
Kn. Your school record was good ; keep it up.
Qn. Laziness retards you.
Kg. You are too versatile.

Spades.

1. Yes.
2. Do not let yourself be overshadowed by others.
3. Nothing better offers as yet.
4. It is too late to change.
5. Jealousy is the chief difficulty for you.
6. To no great extent.
7. You are.
8. You have mistaken your métier.
9. If you used your charm for other ends it would succeed better.
10. You have too many exacting friends.
Kn. You will do better next year.
Qn. You are too easily saddened and discouraged.
Kg. Even so, it is worth the sacrifice.

WHAT IS MY GREAT ATTRIBUTE ?

Diamonds.

1. An understudy of others.
2. Concentration.
3. Perception of the apperceptions of others.
4. Sympathy.
5. Optimism.
6. Capacity for organization.
7. Intelligence.
8. Memory.
9. Sense of justice.
10. Poetic imagery.
Kn. Æsthetic understanding.
Qn. Grit.
Kg. Far-sightedness.

Hearts.

1. Acquisitiveness.
2. Precosity.
3. Stodginess.
4. Trustfulness.
5. A power to prevaricate effectively.
6. Second-sight.
7. Sense of colour.
8. A memory for faces.
9. You are very bland.
10. Carefulness.
Kn. Good judgment.
Qn. Facility in all things.
Kg. Quiescence.

WHAT IS MY GREAT ATTRIBUTE?

Clubs.

1. Love of adventure.
2. Love of animals.
3. Generosity.
4. You are very well meaning.
5. A light touch.
6. Solemnity.
7. Piety.
8. A pleasant wit.
9. Malice well disguised.
10. Vacillation.
Kn. Cunning.
Qn. Graciousness.
Kg. Superstition.

Spades.

1. A morbid streak.
2. You are very clumsy.
3. Gush.
4. Loveableness.
5. Ambition.
6. Exaggeration.
7. Hostility.
8. Defiance.
9. You are a Prodigal.
10. Vanity.
Kn. Common sense.
Qn. The vapours.
Kg. Lethargy.

WILL MY SECRET BE KEPT?

Diamonds.

1. How many know it already?
2. Some suspect, but none are sure.
3. You will take it with you to the grave.
4. You will be basely betrayed.
5. Beware, there are eavesdroppers about.
6. You cannot be too cautious.
7. It does not matter as it is too trivial.
8. You will betray yourself.
9. An accident will disclose it.
10. Your manner causes comment.
Kn. Next week is likely to be dangerous.
Qn. Try not to talk so much.
Kg. You have too good control of yourself to let it be known.

Hearts.

1. Trackers are on your path.
2. No doubt about it. Yes.
3. Something will leak out.
4. When it has ceased to matter, it will be known.
5. You will put them off the scent.
6. By one person only.
7. Walls have ears, take care.
8. Even now it is hinted at.
9. You chose a bad confidant.
10. With luck.
Kn. Published upon the house-tops.
Qn. All too long. Best if it were known.
Kg. When the apples are ripe.

WILL MY SECRET BE KEPT?

Clubs.

1. Years hence.
2. It will leak out shortly.
3. As a sacred oath.
4. The gossips are busy.
5. It is very doubtful.
6. No.
7. You will be questioned about it almost at once.
8. You have done all you can, but to no end.
9. Betrayed.
10. Trust no one.   [yourself.
Kn. You have told too many lies and will contradict
Qn. It is known of.
Kg. No, it will involve others.

Spades.

1. Unless you show fear.
2. The situation grows more and more dangerous for you.
3. Your enemy has discovered it.
4. It is so harmless, why worry?
5. Your conscience is clear, let it be known.
6. Former friends will tell it.
7. It will be extremely well kept.
8. For a long time.
9. Comment is rife.
10. A well-meaning friend will talk too much.
Kn. Rest assured that it will.
Qn. Yes, to your disaster.
Kg. Why have you such a secret? End it.

IS MY FRIEND TRUSTWORTHY?

Diamonds.

1. Sometimes—not always.
2. Yes.
3. No.
4. It is better to be careful.
5. Very dependable.
6. Honest but indiscreet.
7. Will stand by you to the end.
8. Too frivolous to be trusted entirely.
9. Firm as a rock.
10. Changing as the winds.
Kn. Though silent, never forgets.
Qn. Has other fish to fry.
Kg. A good friend makes a good friend.

Hearts.

1. Too critical to be so.
2. Variable.
3. You cannot be quite sure.
4. Essentially so.
5. Except when vexed.
6. Capable of letting you down.
7. No, a secret enemy.
8. Forgetful, not insincere.
9. Very much distressed by your conduct.
10. In everything except money.
Kn. In all save love.
Qn. Such a character has its obvious drawbacks.
Kg. He talks to his wife, be careful.

IS MY FRIEND TRUSTWORTHY?

Clubs.

1. A good friend.
2. Gets too confidential after dinner.
3. A bachelor who marries late is apt to lose his head.
4. Wouldn't hurt you for the world.
5. Don't be disconcerted, he is.
6. Will never betray you.
7. You may well feel uneasy.
8. His wife knows all he knows.
9. When it suits.
10. Always so.
Kn. His tongue is an unruly member.
Qn. True as steel.
Kg. Would give you everything.

Spades.

1. Protests too much.
2. Yes, but will grow very boring.
3. A tireless advocate.
4. Yes, but very jealous.
5. Cares most for the first person singular.
6. Beneath you in rank, but a true friend.
7. Only a sycophant.
8. A better never lived.
9. Stands up for you valiantly.
10. Very critical behind your back.
Kn. Quite indifferent to you.
Qn. Afraid of his family, who dislike you.
Kg. You may trust whole-heartedly.

CONCERNING LOVE

Even in Paradise it is not pleasant to be alone.
EASTERN PROVERB.

SHALL I BE ENGAGED SOON ?

Diamonds.

1. Not as soon as you hope.
2. You have let the years slip by.
3. Your chances are many.
4. Yes, but not to the person you expect.
5. You will be disappointed.
6. Try your luck next month.
7. The omens are not auspicious.
8. Don't rush it.
9. If you write a well-expressed letter.
10. On and off—then off and on.
Kn. Wait until Christmas.
Qn. One sunny afternoon.
Kg. You have but to throw the handkerchief.

Hearts.

1. When opposition is withdrawn.
2. Never, if your sister can prevent it.
3. Yes. To your great satisfaction.
4. Mischief will be made.
5. An enemy will break things off.   [improve.
6. Don't see so much of one another and things will
7. Not for years.
8. Next spring.
9. When the summer comes.
10. When you cross water.
Kn. If you are serious about it.
Qn. Have you tried to make yourself as attractive as
      you might ?
Kg. Are you *sure* it is the right person ?

46

SHALL I BE ENGAGED SOON ?

Clubs.

1. If you became engaged you would lose your nerve.
2. Do you believe in air or bank books ?   [kisses.
3. If you are prepared to live on bread and cheese and
4. You are already pledged elsewhere.
5. What will *she* say if you do ?
6. You will see someone else you like far better.
7. If marriage required a novitiate very few would take the solemn vows.
8. Will your dearest creature be as dear to you in a year's time as now ?
9. You will lose your uncle's money if you do.
10. Be reassured.
Kn. Look before you leap.
Qn. You will have a clandestine engagement.
Kg. What attracts you is a sham.

Spades.

1. Things will prevent it.
2. Several times.
3. First be off with the old love.
4. Expect treachery.
5. Money affairs will hold things up.
6. You are not sufficiently sincere.
7. You are a mocker and will not succeed.   [good.
8. The person you are interested in will go away for
9. Yes, with the approval of all.
10. Directly you do so you will regret it.
Kn. Don't cry because you have not got the moon.
Qn. Affection will increase after marriage.
Kg. Go ahead.

47

DOES —— CARE FOR ME ?

Diamonds.

1. Eternally dreaming of you in absence.
2. No.
3. Not yet.
4. Too selfish to care much.
5. Regards it as a jest.
6. Madly devoted.
7. Less than last year.
8. With silent adoration.
9. Too fickle by nature.
10. Try to forget.
Kn. As a friend.
Qn. Declare yourself and you will discover.
Kg. With increasing warmth.

Hearts.

1. With varying intensity of feeling.
2. Sometimes hates the thought of you.
3. Is trying to forget.
4. Yes, do not misunderstand the long silence.
5. Sorrowfully and without any hope.
6. Not one bit.
7. Better in absence.
8. Only when in need of pecuniary assistance.
9. As a safety valve.
10. Against all better judgments.
Kn. With great loyalty, seeing how trying you are.
Qn. When feeling homesick.
Kg. Adores you always.

DOES —— CARE FOR ME?

Clubs.

1. Do you expect it? Better not.
2. Is temperamentally shallow, and cannot care.
3. Will care when it is too late.
4. Nothing can alter such affection.
5. Has entirely forgotten you already.
6. Is deliberately unfaithful.
7. Finds distraction elsewhere.
8. Cannot be relied upon for long.
9. You mistake kindness for something warmer.
10. Too unimaginative to care.
Kn. Is playing you false.
Qn. Never has and never will.
Kg. In spite of everything, yes.

Spades.

1. Does not feel any too sure.
2. You are one of many.
3. Yes, very dearly.
4. Has departed in a temper.
5. Too jealous and easily upset to care.
6. You are the only pebble on the beach.
7. With increasing intensity.
8. No, it is all pretence.
9. Even though pledged elsewhere.
10. Ever since you first met.
Kn. With a passing fancy.
Qn. Have not the years proved it so?
Kg. Yes, and is very much annoyed that it is so.

HAS MY LETTER FALLEN INTO THE WRONG HANDS?

Diamonds.

1. It will reach you safely.
2. Has been opened and read before it reached you.
3. Has not committed you deeply.
4. Be careful what you write.
5. Is safely under lock and key.
6. Unfortunately, yes.
7. Lost and in the Dead Letter Office.
8. No.
9. Intercepted by an enemy.
10. Only delayed.
Kn. Still in the rack at the Club.
Qn. The Hall Porter has lost it.
Kg. It will reach its destination safely.

Hearts.

1. It only escaped doing so by a miracle.
2. In any case it will be read by others.
3. You should be more careful to whom you write.
4. It did, and that caused all the unpleasantness.
5. You put the wrong address.
6. Be guarded in what you say and it will not matter.
7. Trust no go-between.
8. No, it arrived safely.
9. The trouble began after it was received.
10. It was stolen.
Kn. You were very rash to write as you did.
Qn. Do not keep your letters or they will.
Kg. Always burn them at once.

HAS MY LETTER FALLEN INTO THE WRONG HANDS?

Clubs.

1. It reached its right destination.
2. Has been read by someone you least suspect.
3. There was nothing compromising in any case.
4. You should end all this foolish business of writing notes.
5. The recipient was greatly pleased to get it.
6. Be warned, you will be caught out.
7. The person you write to is so indiscreet.
8. Abstain from pen and ink.
9. Kept, and will give you trouble later on.
10. Blackmail will assuredly follow.

Kn. It is perfectly safe.
Qn. Will be confiscated by your parents.
Kg. Reassure yourself, the danger is past.

Spades.

1. Yes.
2. For a short time, but was returned.
3. Has been sent to the solicitor.
4. Gave a fearful shock to the receiver of it.
5. No one has seen it, but many will.
6. You ought not to write to such indiscreet people.
7. So young and foolish, of course it was left about.
8. No, it is safe.
9. No one is interested in it.
10. Escaped miraculously.

Kn. Very much so.
Qn. Only the hands of a friend.
Kg. It reached its destination safely.

SHALL I MARRY ?

Diamonds.

1. After middle life.
2. Before you are twenty.
3. Never at all.
4. More than once.
5. A marriage *de convenance*.
6. Yes—reluctantly.
7. You will be caught.
8. A rich and happy marriage awaits you.
9. You are too difficult to please.
10. You lack sufficient assurance.
Kn. Alas, you cannot afford to.
Qn. Quite unexpectedly.
Kg. When you have made up your mind.

Hearts.

1. You will have endless opportunities to do so.
2. Yes, and regret it.
3. Out of pique.
4. To please others—a bad reason.
5. Do not be discouraged, you will in the end.
6. You made a mistake to wait so long.
7. It is very doubtful.
8. No, your chance has passed on.
9. After a long engagement.
10. When you escape from present entanglements.
Kn. A poor but happy marriage awaits you.
Qn. April the 1st of next year.
Kg. In due time.

SHALL I MARRY?

Clubs.

1. Yes, fairly soon.
2. An elopement.
3. You will marry and acquire a whole family at the same time.
4. Unfortunately you will marry a very stingy person.
5. You will—a spendthrift.
6. You prefer your liberty.
7. A marriage will be arranged for you.
8. Yes, a foreigner.
9. For money and not love.
10. Yes, in a fit of temper.
Kn. After many postponements.
Qn. A most dramatic affair it will be.
Kg. Yes, but not to the person you think.

Spades.

1. It will be a wild adventure.
2. You will be disappointed in this.
3. Never if you can help it.
4. A very quiet, humdrum affair.
5. When the snow comes.
6. For a second time.
7. Someone you have not yet met.
8. Someone above you in station.
9. You will take the crooked stick.
10. Yes, where you love.
Kn. To ensure an income for yourself.
Qn. Under compulsion.
Kg. On impulse. Beware.

HOW SHALL I RECOGNIZE MY FUTURE WIFE ?

Diamonds.

1. She is a very popular girl.
2. You will meet on the ice rink.
3. Dark and slender.
4. Blonde and gay.
5. Considerably older than you.
6. You will meet in a tram.
7. She is quick-tempered and warm-hearted.
8. By her very pretty feet.
9. She is treating you very badly at present.
10. You have known her for years.
Kn. Your relatives do not smile on the prospect.
Qn. You will begin by disliking her.
Kg. She is the sweetest thing in Baltimore.

Hearts.

1. She will wear black when you meet.
2. She has green eyes.
3. A cousin of your own.
4. She is a Society Queen.
5. By her great beauty.
6. The Cinderella of the family.
7. You will meet her on the rebound.
8. She is singularly dense.
9. Already she influences you.
10. A dazzling meteor blazing for a time in the sky.
Kn. She will lend a listening ear.
Qn. She is very good at games.
Kg. Much made-up.

HOW SHALL I RECOGNIZE MY FUTURE WIFE?

Clubs.

1. She will be recovering from influenza.
2. By her significant silences.
3. She has a loud voice and talks a great deal.
4. She is very decorative.
5. Is like a stained-glass saint.
6. She is being attacked by all your friends.
7. Has caused a great deal of scandal.
8. She is very capricious.
9. Has large brown eyes.
10. Is a violent politician.
Kn. She will alarm you considerably.
Qn. Has a will of her own.
Kg. Elderly and quaint.

Spades.

1. She is a widow.
2. Has just arrived from abroad.
3. Still at school.
4. Is very fond of dogs.
5. Is at present engaged to a friend of yours.
6. She is beautiful and susceptible.
7. The youngest of three sisters.
8. You will meet on a yacht.
9. Your secretary-typist.
10. She openly adores you already.
Kn. You know who she is quite well.
Qn. In a lowly walk in life.
Kg. Very feline.

55

HOW SHALL I RECOGNIZE MY FUTURE HUSBAND ?

Diamonds.

1. Goes to a very bad tailor.
2. He is older than you, but still attractive.
3. Wears a blue serge suit and a bowler hat.
4. In the Civil Service.
5. The Army is his profession.
6. Fond of the sea.
7. A Popular Preacher.
8. Very serious and shy.
9. Wears an eye-glass.
10. Shockingly untidy.
Kn. Young and athletic.
Qn. No one else seems to care for him.
Kg. Your mother disapproves of him.

Hearts.

1. Has a slight stammer.
2. Wears uniform.
3. He is easily shocked.
4. Has a red beard.
5. By his apparent meekness, which is assumed.
6. He speaks several languages.
7. Is a diplomat.
8. You met him in the rain.
9. He has large feet and hands.
10. Clean-shaven and bland.
Kn. By his platitudinous conversation.
Qn. Elderly and clever.
Kg. Has a plump, fair face, open as the day.

HOW SHALL I RECOGNIZE MY FUTURE HUSBAND ?

Clubs.

1. Wears race-glasses.
2. Takes himself very seriously indeed.
3. Expresses himself with difficulty.
4. His family regard him as a waster.
5. Has the nose of a conqueror.
6. A commanding personality.
7. By his violent temper.
8. He is very inaccurate as to facts.
9. The hero of a *cause célèbre*.
10. Very modern indeed.
Kn. A young Apollo.
Qn. A hard-working curate.
Kg. A quiet and sensible man of steady habits.

Spades.

1. Dark and romantic in appearance.
2. Only a boy in years.
3. By his fondness for practical jokes.
4. He is sinister and strange.
5. Never ceases talking.
6. A fighter and too quarrelsome.
7. No one but you appreciates him.
8. He is poor but honest.
9. A son of the soil.
10. Calls a table napkin a serviette.
Kn. Lifts his little finger.too frequently.
Qn. He is contentedly ignorant of all good literature.
Kg. Is a High-brow.

WHY AM I BELOVED? (Lady)

Diamonds.

1. He does not really mean it.
2. For your material advantages.
3. For your charm.
4. That happy laugh.
5. Your good sense appeals to him.
6. Placidity, verging upon dullness, pleases him.
7. You always agree with him.
8. You are his Egeria.
9. Because he wished for somebody just like you.
10. Because you were so good to him.
Kn. You cheered his loneliness.
Qn. You encouraged his hopes.
Kg. For your endless tactfulness.

Hearts.

1. He approves of your views on life.
2. Alas, he loves a certain lady even better.
3. For your conversational powers.
4. Because he is very miserable just now.
5. He thinks it adds lustre to his reputation.
6. Vanity on his part.
7. He depends upon you.
8. For purely selfish reasons.
9. For your beauty.
10. He is sentimental by nature.
Kn. Because you are an heiress.
Qn. He likes clinging ivy.
Kg. He thinks you wonderful.

WHY AM I BELOVED ? (Lady)

Clubs.

1. Because you are good and trusting.
2. Not for your beauty.
3. He thinks you very practical.
4. He wants a good housekeeper.
5. He is tired of change.
6. He feels you to be his mental equal.
7. Because you are young and kittenish.
8. He wants to take you from another.
9. For the sake of variety.
10. He wants a good comrade.
Kn. You have stood by him through so much.
Qn. A mad and passing fancy for you only and no more.
Kg. Out of contradictoriness.

Spades.

1. From long association.
2. Your spirited repartee pleases him.
3. You are the tragic centre of his life.
4. You remind him of his first wife.
5. Because you caught him on the rebound.
6. No one can explain it at all.
7. You fascinate all, why not him ?
8. He likes to be in the fashion.
9. For your fortitude.
10. You bring romance into his life.
Kn. The circumstances under which you met account
     for it.
Qn. He sees in you a darner of socks.
Kg. Youth calls to youth.

59

WHY AM I BELOVED ?   (Gentleman)

Diamonds.

1. Pity's akin to love.
2. You are not beloved, you are respected.
3. Because you are a coming man.
4. It is your hearty manner.
5. She has great faith in your judgments.
6. She prefers quantity to quality.
7. Because everyone else dislikes you.
8. She adores success.
9. Weakness appeals to her.
10. She isn't sure that she does.
Kn. Because you avoid her.
Qn. There is no one else.
Kg. Long habit accounts for it.

Hearts.

1. She likes your grand manner.
2. You are her last chance.
3. She has angled for you for a long time.
4. She hopes to make something of you.
5. She mistakes your stupidity for strong silence.
6. You are such a contrast to your predecessor.
7. Your masterful ways impress her.
8. You have the gift of compliment.
9. She thinks you a celebrity.
10. Her demands are not exacting.
Kn. She feels that you rely on her.
Qn. For your debonair manner.
Kg. Only by way of variety.

WHY AM I BELOVED ? (Gentleman)

Clubs.

1. There are times when she detests you.
2. She is maternally affectionate.
3. Because she is never sure of you.
4. You have tastes in common.
5. Because her people oppose it.
6. " Because you are you," as no doubt she has said.
7. Your youth appeals to her maturity.
8. Because she can trample upon you.
9. She only wants to take you from a friend.
10. She is a man-eater ; beware of her, she loves everyone in turn.
Kn. She is a slave to your will and adores you.
Qn. You know how to manage her.
Kg. She thinks you deeply wronged.

Spades.

1. For that high-handed way you have
2. She admires your sulky charm.
3. Because you take her out so much.
4. She only pretends it.
5. She could listen to you forever.
6. Because weakness appeals to her.
7. She wishes to have a comfortable home.
8. She is too shallow to have a real reason.
9. She looks upon you as her superior.
10. She is Andromeda to your Perseus.
Kn. Your wisdom—of course.
Qn. Because you are so generous.
Kg. For your great goodness.

WHICH OF US WILL RULE THE OTHER ?

Diamonds.

1. You will be under-dog.
2. Pretty level terms.
3. You will find a hard master.
4. Your lot is no worse than that of others.
5. You will get your own way by craft.
6. You will rule every roost.
7. You will learn to dread even a lifted eyebrow.
8. Neither of you ; it will be the Butler.
9. You will govern by charm.
10. All will fear your temper.
Kn. You will assert yourself from time to time.
Qn. You will rule by sulking.
Kg. You will live in perfect harmony together.

Hearts.

1. The balance will waver.
2. Neither ; you will go your own ways.
3. You will, through much plausibility.
4. You will both be ruled by a relative who will live with you.
5. Do not assert yourself too much.
6. You will, by kisses.
7. You are well accustomed to rule already.
8. Bribes will keep things peaceful.
9. Take care, don't drive too hard.
10. Your life-partner will do so by tact.
Kn. There will be a bad break.
Qn. You will hold the purse-strings tight.
Kg. You are led by the nose.

WHICH OF US WILL RULE THE OTHER ?

Clubs.

1. Try to be reasonable and there will be no friction.
2. A reign of terror awaits you.
3. Secretly, you will tremble.
4. You will.
5. By the magic of your smile.
6. If you lean too hard it will lead to deceit.
7. Try to play fair.
8. The odds are even.
9. You take a mean advantage.
10. You are the law-giver.
Kn. You will be forced to obey.
Qn. A perfect compact.
Kg. Learn to bow before the storm.

Spades.

1. You will always be spoilt.
2. You are up against it this time.
3. You are relentless.
4. You will be discouraged and give in.
5. Your lot is that of a door-mat.
6. Take things easy.
7. You will laugh and go your own way unscathed.
8. Your patience will become a proverb.
9. All goes as you want it to.
10. There will be no flies in the honey.
Kn. The air will be full of the cooing of doves.
Qn. Half and half.
Kg. A wise compromise will be made.

HOW MANY TIMES SHALL I FALL IN LOVE?

Diamonds.

1. Once and forever.
2. Every time you go to a new place.
3. Often. With heart-breaking consequences.
4. Once in early and once very late in life.
5. You began in the schoolroom.
6. Never at all.
7. Once, when it is too late.
8. Once against your better judgment.
9. You are fickle and cold-hearted and do not love anyone but yourself.
10. Your fidelity is the admiration of all.
Kn. A lonely life awaits you.
Qn. Often, but in vain.
Kg. You have a true and loyal heart.

Hearts.

1. You are always finding a new star.
2. The last is always the best.
3. Your Irish blood makes you faithful.
4. You are an anchorite.
5. You flit from flower to flower.
6. You will, once too often.
7. Often, but soon over.
8. When it least suits your plans.
9. You will break all records.
10. When you go East.
Kn. You boast and will be punished.
Qn. Take care; your number is up.
Kg. If you go South.

HOW MANY TIMES SHALL I FALL IN LOVE ?

Clubs.

1. You cannot resist dark eyes.
2. Oh ! Those endearing young charms.
3. With one after another.
4. You enjoy doing so.
5. In Normandy.
6. Very unwisely.
7. Disastrously.
8. Wait a year or so.
9. You will walk slowly into it.
10. It will come like a dream and go like a dream.
Kn. You are doing so now.
Qn. Alas, you cannot forget the past.
Kg. Frequently.

Spades.

1. You always love unsuitably.
2. You love an illusion.
3. You have put all that aside for good.
4. No one can keep count.
5. You are too fastidious.
6. For a brief spell.
7. A midsummer madness.
8. Yes, and never recover.
9. You did, long ago.
10. No, you are too shallow.
Kn. On summer seas.
Qn. Twice with the same person.
Kg. You love a memory.

SHALL I BE GIVEN MANY WEDDING GIFTS?

Diamonds.

1. A number of tea-spoons.
2. Yes, bought at an auction.
3. The family diamonds.
4. Several large cheques.
5. Your Aunt's silver tea-pot.
6. Sets of salt-cellars.
7. Presentation trays.
8. You had better buy your own.
9. Many, but all must be returned.
10. A Rolls-Royce car.
Kn. Household goods and gods.
Qn. A number of perfectly useless trifles.
Kg. The family Bible.

Hearts.

1. Few and good.
2. China and plate.
3. A house and a conservatory.
4. A large anonymous gift.
5. A Grand Piano.
6. The family jewels.
7. An American motor-car.
8. A gramophone.
9. You will be given back your former presents to another.
10. A very nice collection of butterflies.
Kn. A token you would rather not have.
Qn. A mascot which will bring you luck.
Kg. An Ideal Home complete with Loud Speaker.

SHALL I BE GIVEN MANY WEDDING GIFTS?

Clubs.

1. Your Aunt will give you a cheque.
2. A few things picked up at Bazaars.
3. Some unconsidered trifles.
4. A parrot who can talk fluently.
5. Books from their Authors.
6. Eastern embroideries from Uncle.
7. Diamonds from the Palais Royal.
8. A great deal of good advice.
9. You will get none.
10. More than you want.
Kn. Nothing you need insure.
Qn. Something to remind you of the past.
Kg. Many, but all useless.

Spades.

1. A tantalus.
2. A family portrait which the family do not appreciate.
3. Several postal orders.
4. Household necessaries.
5. A tea-caddy.
6. Pearls—bought by the yard.
7. An umbrella which you will lose.
8. A cake-stand.
9. A Ukulele.
10. A carpet from Brussels.
Kn. A grandfather clock.
Qn. A wrist-watch.
Kg. A beautifully bound account book.

WILL MY MARRIED LIFE BE HAUNTED BY REGRET ?

Diamonds.

1. There will be a shadowy third.
2. At times.
3. No.
4. Regrets are vain.
5. Put the past behind you for good.
6. You have nothing to regret.
7. Time will heal the wound.
8. Your brooding temperament exaggerates facts.
9. Dry those tears.
10. You are too cynical to care.
Kn. Your memory is a very short one.
Qn. Yes, through your own stupidity.
Kg. You have nothing to fear.

Hearts.

1. No, you will remember nothing.
2. In the winter evenings.
3. When by accident you meet your first love.
4. Occasionally.
5. You like to play with your emotions.
6. For a time.
7. A sentimental shadow occasionally veils the sun.
8. Not after a year.
9. Deeply.
10. Not only by regret, but by something stronger.
Kn. You have good reason to suppose it.
Qn. No ; by apprehension.
Kg. There are no clouds or shadows for you.

WILL MY MARRIED LIFE BE HAUNTED BY REGRET ?

Clubs.

1. If you close the door of memory, all will be well.
2. Don't think about it.
3. Regret will postpone or even prevent your marriage.
4. Yes.
5. You are too heartless to care.
6. That face will haunt you.
7. Do you not richly deserve it ?
8. No, by creditors.
9. To the point of distraction.
10. Keep your head.
Kn. You will lose your nerve.
Qn. You have forgotten all.
Kg. No, you will not marry.

Spades.

1. There is no peace for you.
2. If you have a conscience at all.
3. Not for long.
4. Those eyes will watch and weep.
5. Never mind, it can't be helped.
6. Indeed you will.
7. You never regret.
8. The early years have still their power.
9. Comparatively little.
10. You are too hardened.
Kn. Not unless you are threatened.
Qn. Not with any lasting effect.
Kg. Never. Why should it be ?

WHY IS MY HUSBAND'S CONDUCT SO STRANGE ?

Diamonds.

1. Night clubs.
2. Cocktails.
3. He has been losing money.
4. Be more considerate and things will improve.
5. Change your cook.
6. Overwork.
7. Nerves.
8. Smokes too much.
9. His suspicions are aroused.
10. He loves another.
Kn. After effects of 'flu.
Qn. Boredom.
Kg. Gin.

Hearts.

1. It's the family failing coming to the surface.
2. Ask his cheque book.
3. Watch that fair friend of yours.
4. Jealousy.
5. He is dreadfully worried.
6. A friend has let him down.
7. Cards.
8. The Races.
9. He wishes to go abroad.
10. His peace is threatened.
Kn. He is waiting to hear important news.
Qn. He has conscientious scruples.
Kg. He wishes to go on the stage.

WHY IS MY HUSBAND'S CONDUCT SO STRANGE?

Clubs.

1. Ask the barber.
2. He feels no longer young.
3. Lock the tantalus.
4. He needs a change.
5. A little disturbed in spirit.
6. He has had bad news.
7. He has a guilty secret.
8. Has been prevaricating.
9. Is haunted by his Past.
10. You imagine it.
Kn. He has met someone he likes better, or imagines that he has.
Qn. You have disappointed him sorely.
Kg. He is not prepared to be generous.

Spades.

1. Better not inquire.
2. You will find out to-morrow.
3. Leave well alone.
4. He is deceiving you.
5. He has just encountered his old love.
6. No need for fear.
7. He loves you too well.
8. The sword of Damocles hangs over his head.
9. He has a very defective sense of hearing at times.
10. Something concerning legal matters accounts for it.
Kn. Indigestion.
Qn. Temper.
Kg. Only his usual sulks.

WHY IS MY WIFE'S CONDUCT SO STRANGE?

Diamonds.

1. She needs a change of air.
2. Her dressmaker's bill.
3. Well-founded suspicions.
4. Because she is misunderstood.
5. She wants a new hat.
6. Bridge losses.
7. Trouble with the servants.
8. You talk in your sleep.
9. That gramophone you like so much.
10. She is jealous.
Kn. She is on the verge of hysterics.
Qn. She begins to regret.
Kg. A guilty conscience. She has been faking the housekeeping accounts.

Hearts.

1. She no longer thinks you inspired.
2. She is hiding something from you.
3. Do you really not guess?
4. She finds you antagonistic.
5. Be patient, it will pass.
6. She is deeply hurt.
7. You pay too much attention to other women.
8. She is naturally morose.
9. She has a harmless secret.
10. She wants a bigger allowance.
Kn. She can't bear criticism.
Qn. Her mother has made mischief.
Kg. You refused to let her accept an invitation.

WHY IS MY WIFE'S CONDUCT SO STRANGE ?

Clubs.

1. She is too popular elsewhere.
2. Her heart wanders.
3. She is under the influence of a woman who dislikes you.
4. She adores you. It is only her way of showing it.
5. These little storms will pass.
6. She is very absent-minded.
7. It is her youthfulness.
8. The chauffeur has upset her.
9. Too much jazzing.
10. Too many cinemas.
Kn. She is stage-struck.
Qn. It means nothing.
Kg. She will recover soon.

Spades.

1. She fears she is losing her beauty.
2. Only sulks.
3. She is afraid of you.
4. Prolonged insomnia.
5. You show too little consideration.
6. She dreads your departure.
7. You have spoilt her consistently.
8. She drinks her tea too strong.
9. Gossip.
10. She is asserting herself.
Kn. She is testing you.
Qn. Only a phase which will not last.
Kg. Temper.

WHAT DO MY FRIENDS THINK OF MY ENGAGEMENT ?

Diamonds.

1. They are amazed.
2. Very imprudent.
3. Exactly what they expected.
4. They disapprove.
5. They are delighted.
6. Congratulations on every side.
7. They laugh.
8. They all say " lucky man."
9. They only consider the financial side.
10. Never mind what they say.
Kn. They are resigned.
Qn. They are full of misgivings.
Kg. Everyone is pleased.

Hearts.

1. " Better late than never."
2. That it will end badly.
3. The disparity in age will cause trouble.
4. Nothing could be more suitable.
5. They pity Father's cheque book.
6. That first love is not yet forgotten nor the next come.
7. They are sceptical.
8. That it is a pity.
9. Little short of a miracle.
10. They wish you well.
Kn. A good thing for you, at least.
Qn. What a good-looking couple you will be.
Kg. They hope it may steady you.

WHAT DO MY FRIENDS THINK OF MY ENGAGEMENT?

Clubs.

1. That it serves you right.
2. Very rash.
3. A forlorn hope.
4. All congratulate you.
5. No one has yet bought their present for you.
6. Your last chance.
7. That you are clever to have arrived at it.
8. A little premature.
9. That you are led away by sentiment.
10. That your people arranged it for you.
11. That your former experience should have warned you.
12. That the second family will not like it.
13. They don't envy you.

Spades.

1. They are enchanted.
2. Vastly intrigued.
3. Extremely taken aback.
4. No one expected it.
5. They wonder how you got free to act.
6. With admiration.
7. They envy you your luck.
8. They say it won't come off.
9. On the whole they are shocked.
10. Universal applause.
11. They are genuinely pleased.
12. They admire your.courage.
13. You have startled them considerably.

AM I BLINDED BY LOVE ?

Diamonds.

1. You are. Seek not to see.
2. Not at all ; you see everything too clearly.
3. You prefer it so—wisely.
4. No, you are too intelligent.
5. You are perfectly correct in your judgments.
6. Yes, you are behaving foolishly.
7. It is not Love which blinds you.
8. Yes, but it does not matter.
9. No.
10. Fate will loose the bandage.
Kn. You close your eyes deliberately.
Qn. Nothing can blind you.
Kg. It is important for you to forget.

Hearts.

1. Better so.
2. Wilfully.
3. You desire not to see.
4. Not you !
5. It makes for peace that you are.
6. No, you always suspect everyone.
7. You close your eyes at times.
8. You might alter your judgments were you not.
9. Blinded by selfishness.
10. Indeed you are not.
Kn. Through great consideration.
Qn. Ever so little.
Kg. You are thinking of something else.

AM I BLINDED BY LOVE?

Clubs.

1. You will not remain so.
2. Expect a shock.
3. There is nothing to fear.
4. You are very foolish in this respect.
5. All who love well do not love wisely.
6. Remain contentedly short-sighted.
7. You have eyes like gimlets.
8. There is nothing to see except beauty.
9. Your mind is set upon a different object.
10. No, only dazzled.
Kn. Do not exaggerate; you see well enough.
Qn. You wear rose-coloured spectacles.
Kg. You never will be.

Spades.

1. Kindness makes you so.
2. Remain so or your vanity will suffer.
3. Not at all.
4. Open your eyes and face facts.
5. To the blind all things are sudden.
6. Greatly to your own advantage.
7. Leave it at that.
8. All is well.
9. No, you do not appreciate what you have.
10. In a special manner.
Kn. Occasionally.
Qn. You were, but are so no longer.
Kg. Nothing is hidden, nor need it be.

WHAT WILL FIRST STRIKE ME ABOUT THE PERSON I AM TO MARRY?

Diamonds.

1. Heartiness.
2. Mournfulness.
3. A fine Patriotism.
4. Love of games.
5. The magic of a smile.
6. Eyes of most unholy blue.
7. Piano fingers.
8. A good profile.
9. A certain defiance.
10. Loud taste in clothes.
Kn. A high colour.
Qn. Red-gold hair.
Kg. A determination to do all the talking.

Hearts.

1. Down-cast eyes.
2. A very smart appearance.
3. You will be anything but well impressed.
4. Tremendous self-assurance.
5. An aristocratic calm.
6. Eyes of a different colour.
7. Dimples.
8. Raven hair.
9. A very cold and formal manner.
10. Something bird-like.
Kn. That thrilling personality.
Qn. A silvery voice.
Kg. A slim and graceful poise.

VHAT WILL FIRST STRIKE ME ABOUT THE PERSON I AM TO MARRY?

Clubs.

1. Your first impression is hostile.
2. After a time you will grow used to a squint.
3. A gushing manner.
4. You will be frankly bored.
5. Undeniable beauty.
6. Strong silence.
7. Sympathy.
8. Happiness of temperament.
9. Buoyancy.
10. Friendliness.
Kn. A steady stare.
Qn. A determination to become introduced to you.
Kg. A charm of weakness.

Spades.

1. That southern charm you know so well.
2. Shyness amounting to gaucherie.
3. Pushfulness.
4. A stormy silence.
5. A sort of worldly wisdom.
6. Eagerness.
7. Out-spokenness.
8. An effect of wealth.
9. Good manners.
10. Something wrong somewhere.
Kn. Youth and elegance.
Qn. Depression.
Kg. That all-conquering smile.

CONCERNING CHANCE

He who waits a good day will get a good day.
IRISH PROVERB.

F

WHAT ARE MY LUCKY NUMBERS ?

Diamonds.

1. 4. 32.
2. 26. 1.
3. 3. 4. 7. 20.
4. 17.
5. 21. 7. 53.
6. 9. 8. 5.
7. 2. 11.
8. 13.
9. 44. 10.
10. 40. 2.
Kn. 29. 35.
Qn. 23. 11.
Kg. 7. 3. 9.

Hearts.

1. 10.
2. 6. 26.
3. 40.
4. 47.
5. 7.
6. 3. 13. 23.
7. 28.
8. 30.
9. 9.
10. 1. 4.
Kn. 17.
Qn. 21.
Kg. 6. 8. 12.

WHAT ARE MY LUCKY NUMBERS?

Clubs.

1. 8. 3.
2. 34.
3. 22.
4. 16.
5. 19.
6. 4. 5. 10.
7. 21.
8. All uneven numbers.
9. 50.
10. 7. 2.
Kn. 18.
Qn. 39.
Kg. 1.

Spades.

1. 4.
2. 26.
3. 7.
4. 9.
5. 18.
6. 12.
7. 13.
8. 44.
9. 16.
10. 12.
Kn. You have none. Back a Zero chance.
Qn. 16.
Kg. 11.

WHAT IS MY LUCKY MONTH ?

Diamonds.

1. February—towards end.
2. Never undertake business affairs in April.
3. June, for you.
4. If for matters of love, May ; otherwise wait until November. [best.
5. Nothing is very propitious this year, but July is
6. For sea voyages or journeys, September.
7. At all costs make no final decisions during the month of October.
8. December holds luck for you.
9. A hopeful and happy month awaits you in the Autumn season.
10. January.
Kn. The mad month of March.
Qn. A good change comes in August.
Kg. June.

Hearts.

1. March.
2. Late December.
3. Mid-May.
4. October the gypsy month.
5. July.
6. May when the cuckoo calls.
7. January.
8. August, the latter half.
9. February at its worst.
10. June.
Kn. April for folly.
Qn. Midsummer.
Kg. September.

WHAT IS MY LUCKY MONTH ?

Clubs.

1. Always act quickly in November.
2. Round about Easter.
3. Within the octave of All Souls.
4. March.
5. When the snows are down.
6. When the swallows build.
7. With the fall of the leaf.
8. May.
9. December.
10. With the primroses.
Kn. When all is bleak and cold.
Qn. July.
Kg. At the year's end.

Spades.

1. Lilac time.
2. January.
3. Midsummer.
4. With the cold dew.
5. Daffodil month.
6. May.
7. December.
8. When ice is over the waters.
9. July.
10. The early Autumn.
Kn. February.
Qn. September.
Kg. Near Christmas.

WILL MY PRESENT LUCK CHANGE ?

Diamonds.

1. In a month's time at most.
2. A short journey by road will alter everything.
3. For the better, quite soon.
4. The act of a friend will alter things.
5. Yes, through your own blindness.
6. Great good fortune awaits you when least you expect it.
7. Be careful, you walk amid quicksands.
8. Your luck will hold.
9. Do not grieve, all is well.
10. Swift as a storm disaster nears you.
Kn. It depends upon yourself.
Qn. Time is on your side.
Kg. You are in for a Grand Slam.

Hearts.

1. Unless your timidity prevents it.
2. Things will be worse before it does.
3. Do nothing until you have been away.
4. Yes, with magnificent results.
5. Don't be depressed.   It has changed now.
6. You are coming near a heavy test.
7. It will, for the better.
8. Have no fear, all is well.
9. Go on and prosper.
10. It is in the balance.
Kn. With a flourish of trumpets.
Qn. Patience, it soon will.
Kg. If you have fortitude.

WILL MY PRESENT LUCK CHANGE?

Clubs.

1. Through the agency of an unknown helper.
2. Not until you are more sensible.
3. You must first assert yourself.
4. You will defeat a plot against you.
5. The clouds will break ere long.
6. Have no misgivings as to this.
7. Take it lightly and it will.
8. Before sunset.
9. Within a month or even less.
10. If you listen to the good advice you have been given.
Kn. All is bright ahead of you.
Qn. You are only suffering from a slight set-back.
Kg. Courage, you are sure to succeed.

Spades.

1. Unquestionably, yes.
2. Best leave it alone.
3. Again and yet again.
4. Try something different.
5. The fall of the cards is against you.
6. It is your sole chance of success.
7. Try a fresh method and show tact.
8. You are advised to desist.
9. There will be no second opportunity.
10. Wait a year.
Kn. Reflect before a fresh attempt.
Qn. Certainly, for you will progress.
Kg. An attempt must be made and you will be rewarded.

HAS —— A LUCKY OR AN UNLUCKY INFLUENCE OVER ME?

Diamonds.

1. Avoid that person.
2. An influence gained by flattery.
3. The best influence in your life.
4. On no account arrange a journey together.
5. A source of hope and comfort.
6. Such a beautiful character can only assist and inspire.
7. Will certainly abuse your confidence.
8. No influence at all.
9. Only a passing one.
10. For evil.
Kn. An exasperating one.
Qn. You are nothing but an echo.
Kg. It is you who exercise all the influence.

Hearts.

1. Desires to be helpful to you.
2. Cramps your style.
3. Imitates you to the point of folly.
4. You fear their ridicule.
5. Pay no heed to this person.
6. In special cases.
7. It is regarded as unfortunate.
8. The very best possible.
9. Like sunlight.
10. Highly improving.
Kn. Only to beguile your time.
Qn. An uncomfortable one.
Kg. Gives you a weighty sense of responsibility.

HAS —— A LUCKY OR AN UNLUCKY INFLUENCE OVER ME?

Clubs.

1. A very deceitful one.
2. Encourages you to mutiny.
3. Thrilling.
4. Highly stimulating.
5. For your good.
6. Only to distract and dismay.
7. Makes you fear the future.
8. Peaceful and consoling.
9. Entirely sentimental.
10. Appeals to your generosity.
Kn. Leaves you quite cold.
Qn. None.
Kg. A softening one.

Spades.

1. Very dismal.
2. Incites you to rash action.
3. Beware, danger lurks in this.
4. For your welfare.
5. Gays you up when you need it.
6. Inclines you to extravagance.
7. Cheerful.
8. Very sinister.
9. Best escape it.
10. Quiets your nerves.
Kn. Helpful.
Qn. A beautiful one.
Kg. Acid to a degree.

WILL THE PLAN I HAVE IN MIND SUCCEED ?

Diamonds.

1. It will in part only.
2. No, you will abandon it for a better.
3. Those concerned in it are as fickle as the waves of the sea.
4. It is very undesirable that it should.
5. Your own good sense will cause you to drop it.
6. It will meet with phenomenal success.
7. Take care, take care, there is a snake in the grass.
8. You will be well satisfied.
9. A chain of events, unknown to you, is bringing the fulfilment daily nearer.
10. Keep your own counsel and it will.
Kn. Over-enthusiasm will mar the plan.
Qn. When you have given up all hope.
Kg. On its own merits, yes.

Hearts.

1. Very unexpectedly indeed.
2. Through the good offices of a friend.
3. No.
4. It will be delayed.
5. It will be shattered to bits.
6. It is only a dream.
7. Bringing you wonderful joy and rest.
8. If the others do their part.
9. To-morrow will tell.
10. You conquer all and will again.
Kn. You stand in your own light.
Qn. If you can raise the wind.
Kg. Unfortunately, yes.

WILL THE PLAN I HAVE IN MIND SUCCEED ?

Clubs.

1. In a measure.
2. As a result of really hard work.
3. It is opposed in a high quarter.
4. If you approach it simply.
5. Talk will ruin it.
6. If you appear indifferent.
7. See that you create a good impression and it will.
8. It all turns on a whim.
9. Forsake it, or like the asp it will poison you.
10. It will blossom like a rose.
Kn. In the winter of the year.
Qn. Across water and not here.
Kg. Later on in life.

Spades.

1. Next summer.
2. You will be offered something better.
3. You make so many and none come off, nor will they.
4. When all is dark.
5. Love will assist it.
6. Hold fast to it.
7. Before long.
8. No ray of hope.
9. A sweet change is near.
10. With great harmony.
Kn. Only at the last gasp.
Qn. For your heirs.
Kg. In the Far East.

SHALL I RECEIVE THE LETTER I EXPECT?

Diamonds.

1. Yes, blotted with tears.
2. Illness has delayed it.
3. Yes, almost directly.
4. With some misgivings when you do.
5. Yes, it brings you joyful news.
6. With an enclosure as well.
7. It will come, and give you cause for thought.
8. When you no longer expect it.
9. It has been read by a scoffer.
10. The mail has been delayed.
Kn. Already it is in the postman's bag.
Qn. The person to whom it was entrusted has forgotten to post it.
Kg. In the next few days.

Hearts.

1. It has not yet been written.
2. Some other mind dictated it, but it will come.
3. No, a telegram instead.
4. After the wedding.
5. No, there has been an accident.
6. As you did not answer the last, you will not.
7. There is likely to be a long delay.
8. Indolence is the cause.
9. Yes, an angry one.
10. You will, pressing for payment.
Kn. Such a nice one.
Qn. It will alter your outlook on life.
Kg. Full of wise advice.

SHALL I RECEIVE THE LETTER I EXPECT?

Clubs.

1. Sore trouble in the many pages.
2. Oh, do try and cease writing yourself!
3. By the early post.
4. Very satisfactory.
5. A gallant composition when you get it.
6. The news will disappoint you.
7. It contains rejected addresses.
8. It will convey deep regret.
9. You have ceased to expect it.
10. Mischief has been made.
Kn. It has been stolen.
Qn. Full of promises.
Kg. A very amusing one indeed.

Spades.

1. Yes, yet another to add to your collection.
2. Only a postcard.
3. The letter you dream of is coming to you.
4. It uplifts you upon golden wings.
5. Full of love for you.
6. A very unpleasant one indeed.
7. Telling you something that will make you shiver.
8. A good friend has written.
9. By the second post.
10. With a warning in it.
Kn. A very successful reply.
Qn. Not the one you expect.
Kg., It will come years too late.

IS —— HAPPY OR UNHAPPY ?

Diamonds.

1. You are the cause of the sadness.
2. Simply indifferent and callous.
3. Happy, but not for the reason you think.
4. Enjoying life with great zest.
5. Very lonely.
6. Feeling very much better.
7. Not without distractions.
8. Sorely tried.
9. Making the best of things.
10. That you will never know.
Kn. Gloomy.
Qn. In a mad whirl of gaiety.
Kg. Serene and exalted.

Hearts.

1. Went to bed feeling very merry.
2. An uneasy conscience disturbs the subject of your thoughts.
3. Getting over it.
4. Need you ask ?
5. Only just alive and far from happy.
6. Bearing up.
7. Seeking change and distraction.
8. Comatose.
9. Sulking heavily.
10. Keeping on smiling.
Kn. Very much occupied by someone else.
Qn. Has many regrets.
Kg. Will survive it.

94

IS —— HAPPY OR UNHAPPY?

Clubs.

1. Missing you badly.
2. Restored to health and spirits.
3. Sitting up and taking notice.
4. Dramatically heartbroken.
5. Facing life bravely.
6. In two minds.
7. Very home-sick.
8. Boring everyone as usual.
9. In wild spirits.
10. Counting the cost.
11. Thinking it over.
12. Paying a heavy reckoning.
13. Quietly determined to do something desperate.

Spades.

1. Very cheerful indeed.
2. Disgruntled.
3. Enjoying the sunshine.
4. In deep contemplation.
5. Composing verses.
6. Making a final decision.
7. Very much upset on account of a deserved snub.
8. Waiting in vain.
9. Sadder and no wiser.
10. Full of envy.
11. Much gnashing of teeth is going on there.
12. Looking very foolish indeed.
13. In a fine frenzy.

WILL MY JOURNEY BE PROSPEROUS?

Diamonds.

1. If you start in a lucky hour.
2. Unless you are forced to delay it.
3. Once you cross water.
4. There is something menacing you.
5. Very prosperous.
6. Gay and altogether delightful.
7. Pleasures and palaces await you.
8. You will return wiser than you started.
9. If you go alone.
10. Be careful not to make undesirable friends.
Kn. I fear it will not.
Qn. Watch your travelling companions for the first day.
Kg. All the auspices are favourable to you.

Hearts.

1. Not with regard to the weather.
2. Moderately so.
3. It depends upon a man concerned with you.
4. You will be tremendously successful.
5. In every respect.
6. Temper will mar it.
7. Stormy.
8. Fair to moderate.
9. A very ticklish business indeed.
10. Success greets you.
Kn. You will be sorely vexed.
Qn. Partly so.
Kg. Excellent for you.

WILL MY JOURNEY BE PROSPEROUS?

Clubs.

1. Very important, though you know it not.
2. Not for those you go with.
3. Yes.
4. For money affairs.
5. Your journey will end in a lovers' meeting.
6. Short but sweet.
7. Fate smiles upon it.
8. Take care, there is danger.
9. With a little discretion, it will.
10. No, you will be very uncomfortable.
Kn. On reaching your destination you will get a shock.
Qn. Highly fortunate.
Kg. You will lose your luggage.

Spades.

1. There will be a fracas during the trip.
2. Pleasant.
3. Quite sufficiently happy for you.
4. Don't be so easily put out by delays.
5. Go cautiously.
6. Better stay at home.
7. Great changes await you.
8. Pleasure will be certain, if not profit.
9. Do be careful.
10. You are too difficult to make a good traveller.
Kn. You will feel better when you start.
Qn. You are likely to be disappointed.
Kg. Very good in all respects.

WHOM SHOULD I AVOID?

Diamonds.

1. A man with a limp.
2. Be warned against red hair.
3. Someone whose eyebrows join.
4. A middle-aged man with grey eyes and hair.
5. Wears horn-rimmed spectacles.
6. The opposite sex.
7. The doctor.
8. Crystal-gazers.
9. Gamblers.
10. A woman with dark hair.
Kn. One who is near and dear to you.
Qn. Someone you trust.
Kg. Your fair, false friend.

Hearts.

1. All dark-skinned people.
2. Your insolvent friend.
3. A great talker you know well.
4. A young and deceitful person with a charming smile.
5. Someone whose name begins with the letter C.
6. Card-sharpers.
7. Low friends.
8. All your former friends.
9. Those who know your secret.
10. An elderly lady with a strong will.
Kn. Someone in the house with you.
Qn. A gossiping shrew with large teeth.
Kg. The Welsh.

WHOM SHOULD I AVOID ?

Clubs.

1. Your chief adviser.
2. Your *alter ego.*
3. One who loves you.
4. A half-hearted adherent.
5. Your confidential servant.
6. There is no warning for you.
7. An elderly man who haunts you.
8. Foreigners.
9. A woman with a pet dog.
10. Money-lenders.
Kn. A captious critic.
Qn. That would-be " clever " friend.
Kg. A sententious, backbiting female.

Spades.

1. A sentimentalist.
2. Loud speakers of all kinds.
3. A fat man who appears amiable.
4. Quack doctors.
5. Dagos.
6. A spinster who is deeply interested in you.
7. Yogis.
8. An earnest thinker who desires to improve you.
9. A dry cynic who hates you.
10. A strange individual from the East.
Kn. A long-forgotten love.
Qn. Someone you have not met yet.
Kg. Political agents.

AM I IN DANGER?

Diamonds.

1. Insure against fire.
2. Yes, through your lavish generosity.
3. Avoid Continental railway travelling for a time.
4. Be careful on the moving staircase.
5. Yes, unless you change your chauffeur.
6. In no danger. All is well.
7. Only from your own rashness.
8. You must pay attention to your diet.
9. You have powerful friends to protect you.
10. Yes, through a lack of judgment.
Kn. Not if you hold your peace.
Qn. From an old and nearly forgotten enemy.
Kg. You need fear nothing.

Hearts.

1. You were, but it is over.
2. Not if you are moderate.
3. Yes, on the seas.
4. You will have a fall.
5. In danger of loss.
6. No.
7. Jealousy menaces you.
8. There is danger of competition.
9. Indiscreet talk will bring trouble.
10. Be careful in the snow.
Kn. Keep away from a house in the country.
Qn. Through a woman's jealousy.
Kg. Less so as time goes on.

AM I IN DANGER?

Clubs.

1. Be cautious with animals.
2. Keep indoors during thunderstorms.
3. Never eat potted meat sandwiches.
4. Give up that motor-bike.
5. Yes, during the next week.
6. Only from your own temperament.
7. Yes, unless you take exercise.
8. There is no danger near you.
9. Of an asthmatic attack.
10. Yes, because you fear to learn the truth.
Kn. Only in danger of making a hopeless fool of yourself.
Qn. Do what you are advised and all will be well.
Kg. Not in the least.

Spades.

1. Seriously so.
2. The trouble will soon pass for good.
3. There is nothing to dread.
4. Of falling masonry.
5. Your nerves make you so.
6. Avoid hot climates.
7. Wear warmer clothes or you will be.
8. No, you exaggerate things.
9. Of losing your head.
10. Of dentists.
Kn. Of cheating at games, for you will be caught.
Qn. Of repeating scandal.   Don't do it.
Kg. Of a fatal attempt to appear wealthier and cleverer
than you are.

WHAT IS THE CAUSE OF THE TROUBLE IN THE HOUSE ?

Diamonds.

1. The youngest member of the family.
2. A mislaid letter.
3. Shortness of cash.
4. The domestic staff are about to give notice.
5. A clandestine love affair.
6. Something valuable has been lost.
7. Political controversy.
8. Suspicion.
9. Unpunctuality.
10. Tale-bearing.
Kn. A guest who has stayed too long.
Qn. Bills.
Kg. Late hours.

Hearts.

1. Over-sensitiveness.
2. Fear.
3. The family skeleton.
4. Too much champagne.
5. Absence of Master.
6. Atmosphere.
7. Drainage system.
8. Expected burglary.
9. Rattling windows.
10. The bath water doesn't heat.
Kn. Meals are so late.
Qn. A black and angry cloud obscures the light.
Kg. The loud-speaker.

WHAT IS THE CAUSE OF THE TROUBLE IN THE HOUSE?

Clubs.

1. There are too many women there.
2. Clash of opinions.
3. Rivalry.
4. Jealousy.
5. There is no trouble where you are.
6. An old antagonism.
7. The staff-work is bad.
8. Silent opposition.
9. A broken promise.
10. That awful altruism of yours.
Kn. Over-conscientiousness.
Qn. Vanity.
Kg. Depression.

Spades.

1. Discontent.
2. The vapours.
3. Unrequited affection.
4. The weather.
5. A badly needed change.
6. The incursion of a foreign body.
7. Slackness.
8. Noise.
9. You attract too many people.
10. They all want the car to go to different places.
Kn. Seek not to know.
Qn. Someone is in a " clothes-rage."
Kg. A secret plot.

WHAT OPINION WILL MEN HAVE OF ME?
(Lady)

Diamonds.

1. That you are too clever by half.
2. They believe in your integrity.
3. They think you well-meaning and kind.
4. They deeply respect your opinion.
5. They are afraid of you.
6. You fascinate them.
7. They rely on you for sympathy.
8. They depend on your advice.
9. None too good.
10. A good comrade.
Kn. They find you intensely interesting.
Qn. They admire your high principles.
Kg. They appreciate your courage and audacity.

Hearts.

1. They admire your languorous charm.
2. They fear your tongue.
3. They think you snub them.
4. You are too eager to please.
5. A moderately good one.
6. Unexceptionable.
7. That you can be very catty at times.
8. In awe of you.
9. That you are a dream.
10. They are hostile.
Kn. A good hostess.
Qn. A woman with a purpose.
Kg. That you are very beautiful.

WHAT OPINION WILL MEN HAVE OF ME?
(Lady)

Clubs.

1. They run before you.
2. Shallow.
3. Very versatile.
4. Very, very wise.
5. A few like you.
6. They follow you like a flock of sheep.
7. Most of them are foolish about you.
8. You are too wilful to please them.
9. They realize your weakness for chocolate.
10. They yearn to smack you.
Kn. Unreliable.
Qn. They are truly sorry for you.
Kg. A perfect saint.

Spades.

1. Deeply wronged.
2. Frivolous.
3. Your icy manner alienates them.
4. Great fun.
5. They fear to burn their wings.
6. They admire you from a distance.
7. They make the best of you.
8. They don't think of you at all.
9. They kneel at your feet.
10. You puzzle them.
Kn. Would like to know you better.
Qn. That you mean well.
Kg. That you lay it on too thick.

WHAT OPINION WILL WOMEN HAVE OF ME?
(Gentleman)

Diamonds.

1. Rather a dear.
2. A sinister figure.
3. Terribly attractive.
4. To be avoided.
5. Very wild.
6. Mediocre.
7. Thoroughly domesticated.
8. Would make a good husband for someone else.
9. A good friend.
10. They ask your advice—but never take it.
Kn. A good sort.
Qn. A cave-man.
Kg. They all adore you.

Hearts.

1. They wonder.
2. They wish you would go away.
3. That you are generous.
4. Very brave.
5. A cynic.
6. Too analytical to please them.
7. Dark and dangerous.
8. Mysterious.
9. Very cheerful.
10. Extremely nice.
Kn. They wish you would talk more.
Qn. They rave about you.
Kg. You inspire them.

WHAT OPINION WILL WOMEN HAVE OF ME?
(Gentleman)

Clubs.

1. A great catch.
2. Lofty in manner.
3. You put on too many airs.
4. Very complex.
5. Quite harmless.
6. They like you better and better.
7. Horribly pampered.
8. Very untruthful.
9. A thoroughly bad man.
10. Too restless.
Kn. Very severe.
Qn. Stingy.
Kg. An amiable idiot.

Spades.

1. Fantastic.
2. So conscientious.
3. They dislike your silent sneer.
4. They all love you.
5. A roué.
6. Of the Corsair type.
7. Too much of the play-actor.
8. Unreliable.
9. Almost too fascinating.
10. You enslave them one and all, old or young.
Kn. Very matter-of-fact.
Qn. Inscrutable.
Kg. You terrify them.

WILL THE SICK PERSON RECOVER ?

Diamonds.

1. Yes.
2. After a week of anxiety.
3. The illness is purely imaginary.
4. You will have good news.
5. The trouble is different to what is supposed.
6. Change of air will work wonders.
7. If the patient is sensible.
8. A matter for good nursing.
9. There will be a long convalescence.
10. Cheerful surroundings will help.
Kn. Already on the mend.
Qn. You must not despair.
Kg. While there's life there's hope.

Hearts.

1. Not unless more tractable and obedient.
2. Under brighter skies.
3. In due time.
4. Quite soon.
5. After a good night's sleep.
6. Take a tonic.
7. Rapidly.
8. By a miracle.
9. Too much fuss at present.
10. Be patient and things will mend.
Kn. A day or two will alter things for the better.
Qn. Slowly coming round.
Kg. Already on the mend.

WILL THE SICK PERSON RECOVER?

Clubs.

1. Much improved already.
2. Yes.
3. Gradually.
4. Rest is all that is necessary.
5. Lively surroundings will assist.
6. All will be well.
7. A matter of will-power.
8. Fear nothing.
9. It is not serious.
10. Only a trifling indisposition.
Kn. Cheer up, it will not last.
Qn. The strain is lessening.
Kg. Growing gradually stronger.

Spades.

1. The shadow is withdrawing slowly.
2. The crisis is past.
3. Health is returning gradually.
4. A long battle to win.
5. Time will help and heal.
6. Sooner even than you hope.
7. Through a sudden change for the better.
8. Do not despair if things are worse for a time.
9. There is nothing the matter.
10. Mountain air will be of great service.
Kn. Should diet more carefully.
Qn. The next news will be better.
Kg. Recovery is certain.

SHALL I BE LUCKY TO-MORROW?

Diamonds.

1. Not altogether.
2. Yes.
3. Try to be patient.
4. The auguries are good.
5. All promises well.
6. Do not be too confident.
7. By the active assistance of a friend.
8. You are in for a strange experience.
9. Partially so.
10. Good luck awaits you.
Kn. Be quiet and wait a little longer.
Qn. To-morrow your fate changes.
Kg. Beware of a new acquaintance.

Hearts.

1. Up to a point.
2. A lame man will call at the house and bring a change.
3. Go nowhere by train.
4. Do not walk alone.
5. Watch for an adventure.
6. Be careful for a day or two.
7. Decidedly.
8. You will meet the one you most desire to see.
9. If dining out, leave early.
10. Don't do anything rash, it's a bad day.
Kn. Yes.
Qn. Good for business matters.
Kg. Indirectly.

SHALL I BE LUCKY TO-MORROW ?

Clubs.

1. Leave well alone to-morrow.
2. Beware of walking under ladders.
3. Very lucky for travelling.
4. Moderately good luck.
5. A negative day.
6. Yes, for letters.
7. Make no plan ; it will fail.
8. An unexpected guest will cheer you greatly.
9. You ought to be.
10. Keep away from water.
Kn. You will succeed.
Qn. Brightening prospects await you.
Kg. Do not be discouraged by a small set-back.

Spades.

1. Aim high.
2. Go carefully.
3. For all things concerning chance, yes.
4. Towards night luck improves.
5. In love, yes.
6. Let slumbering dogs lie.
7. To-morrow will be difficult for you.
8. A day of happy events.
9. If you get up very early.
10. Seek not to disturb the peace.
Kn. Nothing important either way.
Qn. The chance of a lifetime will come.
Kg. Keep your head and you will be the chosen one.

THE LAST LAP

Man's life is like an egg in the hands of a child.

ROUMANIAN PROVERB.

H

WILL MY OLD AGE BE PEACEFUL ?

Diamonds.

1. No, you are too restless.
2. Chequered.
3. A late marriage will make it difficult.
4. Yes, except for gout.
5. Very much so.
6. Contrary winds will blow you out of harbour.
7. You will be troubled by musical neighbours.
8. Like a pleasant dream.
9. Very prosperous indeed.
10. Most of your luck comes late.
Kn. Your own calm will create calm.
Qn. If you do not fuss.
Kg. You will work to the last.

Hearts.

1. Highly dramatic.
2. Like a meteor.
3. Not entirely so.
4. You began as a tripper and will end as a pilgrim.
5. After forty the storm blows hard.
6. You will turn over a new leaf.
7. Your sharp tongue will make it a battle-ground.
8. Your beauty is of the fadeless sort.
9. Amusing at all times, even in age.
10. You will never lose your enthusiasm.
Kn. That cannot be.
Qn. You will grow very stout and placid.
Kg. Much tea-drinking and scandal will entertain you.

WILL MY OLD AGE BE PEACEFUL?

Clubs.

1. You will always be surrounded by affection.
2. A railway carriage is your home.
3. Very uneventful.
4. Happy, if dull.
5. Very peaceful in a garden of flowers.
6. Respected and respectable.
7. A Law-giver whom all fear.
8. Terribly garrulous.
9. Gouty and grim.
10. Your happy disposition ensures it.

Kn. No.
Qn. Variable.
Kg. Exquisitely happy.

Spades.

1. Full of memories and memoirs.
2. You will often regret the past.
3. You will find no listener for the tale of your woes.
4. Gracious and fair.
5. That of a discredited politician.
6. How soon the world will forget you.
7. The reward of a noble life.
8. That of a wanderer.
9. No grumbler is ever peaceful.
10. Full of sunshine.

Kn. You will not age well.
Qn. There is a fear that you will be prosy.
Kg. All will love you, as ever.

SHALL I BE BELOVED IN AGE?

Diamonds.

1. With one notable exception.
2. Yes, if you also keep your temper.
3. It is doubtful.
4. Not if you see too much of them.
5. Mischief will be made.
6. The one you value most will love you faithfully.
7. Yes, in spite of much.
8. Until the end.
9. Your friends are almost fanatically faithful to you.
10. Yes, however badly you treat them.
Kn. One friend alone will be loyal.
Qn. You always make fresh friends.
Kg. No one ever forgets you.

Hearts.

1. Those friends you made in middle life will remain.
2. Unless you change, you will not.
3. Deeply so.
4. One will come and go, and, in the end, return.
5. Some will stick to you.
6. You have tried them too high.
7. Your mocking spirit alienates others.
8. Yes.
9. By the friends of your school-days.
10. Undoubtedly you will.
Kn. You are the honey-pot.
Qn. Forever.
Kg. No, people are bored already.

SHALL I BE BELOVED IN AGE ?

Clubs.

1. Even in a bath-chair.
2. If you mellow with time.
3. Your generosity will make it sure.
4. Not unless your temper improves.
5. By some.
6. If you retain your sense of humour.
7. Yes, if you are cheerful.
8. You are too self-centred.
9. As in youth, so in age.   [variety.
10. Age cannot wither nor custom stale your infinite
Kn. The morbid streak in you isolates you.
Qn. You have ever been and will remain a tower of strength to all who know you.
Kg. Yes, but you must pay for it.

Spades.

1. If you desire so to be.
2. No, you are too autocratic.
3. If you interfere less.
4. You will be far more charming then than now.
5. You will rise to giddy heights and be much sought after.
6. You give too much advice.
7. You will be too antagonistic to the young.
8. Adored by the Bourgeoisie.
9. You are too indifferent.
10. You inspire great affection.
Kn. By animals and children.
Qn. Yes, because you are a good sport.
Kg. By elderly ladies and cats.

AGAINST WHAT AM I CHIEFLY WARNED ?

Diamonds.

1. Flying.
2. Port.
3. Cards.
4. Drugs.
5. Cigarettes.
6. Racing.
7. Gossip.
8. Deceit.
9. Infection.
10. Marriage.
Kn. Solicitors.
Qn. Train journeys.
Kg. You are immune.

Hearts.

1. Water.
2. Bearded men.
3. Mountain climbing.
4. Sentiment.
5. Superstition.
6. Trying to be clever.
7. Self-seeking.
8. Burglars.
9. Idle talk.
10. Bribes.
Kn. The family curse.
Qn. Avoir-du-pois.
Kg. Cats.

AGAINST WHAT AM I CHIEFLY WARNED ?

Clubs.

1. Idleness.
2. Bad company.
3. Sunstroke.
4. Horses.
5. Land-slides.
6. Ghosts.
7. Women.
8. Jealousy.
9. Matrimony.
10. Slander.
Kn. False hopes.
Qn. Levity.
Kg. Relatives.

Spades.

1. Change of mind.
2. Fancy balls, where there is great danger to you.
3. Self-assurance.
4. Lonely walks.
5. Colds in the head.
6. Futility.
7. Wet feet.
8. A dark woman.
9. Lightning.
10. Ponds.
Kn. Unripe fruit.
Qn. Dissipation.
Kg. Rash judgments.

IN WHAT PART OF THE WORLD SHALL I LIVE ?

Diamonds.

1. A mountainous country.
2. Southern skies.
3. In a large city.
4. Deep in the country.
5. Near a lake or pool.
6. On a hill-side.
7. In a manufacturing district.
8. You are a nomad.
9. Chiefly abroad.
10. In a University town.
Kn. In the suburbs.
Qn. On an island.
Kg. Near a great wooded park.

Hearts.

1. On an Irish shore.
2. South.
3. In a very cold climate.
4. Near London.
5. You will move every few years.
6. " Peacehaven " will be your home.
7. East Coast.
8. A bungalow on the River.
9. Near great pine woods.
10. Under snow hills.
Kn. You will try Mexico.
Qn. A castle in Spain.
Kg. Under Indian skies.

IN WHAT PART OF THE WORLD SHALL I LIVE ?

Clubs.

1. Europe.
2. Roughing it in Kenya.
3. Philadelphia.
4. North Scotland.
5. The Lake District.
6. Near the Broads.
7. Canada.
8. Wild Wales.
9. An ancient town.
10. Across the Atlantic.
Kn. You will take a different nationality.
Qn. A long way from here.
Kg. Devon.

Spades.

1. Near the sea.
2. Meridional.
3. Yorkshire.
4. British Isles.
5. Island life awaits you.
6. A caravan, for you are a gypsy.
7. Asia.
8. Fen country.
9. On high ground.
10. The Veldt.
Kn. Suburbia.
Qn. Land's End.
Kg. The Carpathians.

WHAT WILL MY HOME BE LIKE?

Diamonds.

1. Built for pleasure and for state.
2. A good Georgian house.
3. Modern architecture.
4. A charming cottage.
5. A flat.
6. You will have a variety of residences.
7. A grey house by the sea.
8. Too large to keep up properly.
9. You will live in hotels.
10. A château.
Kn. A boarding house.
Qn. Bare and uncomfortable.
Kg. An Ideal Home.

Hearts.

1. A ghost-haunted pile.
2. A country rectory.
3. A semi-detached villa.
4. A very large dwelling owned by Government.
5. A peaceful cottage.
6. You will be a P. G.
7. A railway carriage.
8. Green mansions.
9. Small, but comfortable.
10. A ramshackle house.
Kn. A farmstead.
Qn. Like Heaven.
Kg. Lordly indeed !

WHAT WILL MY HOME BE LIKE?

Clubs.

 1. Like an illustration out of *Colour*.
 2. Very uncomfortable, but true to period.
 3. Vulgar.
 4. A studio.
 5. Very bare.
 6. Delightful.
 7. Horribly cold.
 8. Solid and ugly.
 9. A makeshift.
10. Stucco.
Kn. Washed by waters.
Qn. A white house in a row.
Kg. A cottage of gentility.

Spades.

 1. Opulent.
 2. Impressive.
 3. The gates of the avenue are very fine.
 4. A real Home.
 5. Satisfying.
 6. Like a doll's house.
 7. Very attractive.
 8. High on a hill.
 9. A renovated ruin.
10. A Feudal castle.
Kn. Just a lean-to.
Qn. A shack in the wilds.
Kg. A mountain tent ill-pitched and lonely.

SHALL I BE RICH OR POOR ?

Diamonds.

1. Moderate means.
2. You will know vicissitudes.
3. Great fortune which comes by chance.
4. Enough and something over.
5. You will pass through a lean time.
6. Rich by inheritance.
7. Your frugal tastes will be satisfied.
8. Your own endeavours will give you a sufficiency.
9. As a result of a kind deed you will inherit a vast fortune.
10. You will lose your all'gambling.
Kn. Be thrifty and you will never want.
Qn. Your own energy will carry you far.
Kg. Very rich.

Hearts.

1. After years, very rich.
2. Poverty has no fears for you.
3. Ample fortune.
4. Curb your extravagance and you will have enough.
5. You will have to borrow.
6. Work will bring you a good income.
7. Fluctuating fortunes.
8. Poor.
9. You will be rich and regret it.
10. A super-taxer.
Kn. All you get you spend.
Qn. Not quite enough.
Kg. You will lose money.

SHALL I BE RICH OR POOR?

Clubs.

1. Wealth for you.
2. House property by inheritance.
3. You will succeed in land dealings.
4. Streets will be named after you.
5. Surprisingly wealthy.
6. Dire poverty.
7. A change for the better after a short time.
8. Riches.
9. You will embrace Poverty and transform it.
10. A very happy medium.
Kn. Prosperous.
Qn. Adequate means.
Kg. A superfluity.

Spades.

1. Nothing over.
2. You will have nothing to bequeath.
3. Passing rich.
4. Happily provided for.
5. Never at a loss for a fiver.
6. Out of debt and out of danger.
7. You are a good manager and will do well.
8. You will lose everything.
9. Sometimes one, sometimes the other.
10. You will gain wealth.
Kn. Rich only to squander.
Qn. Enough for two.
Kg. Lasting prosperity is yours.

Breinigsville, PA USA
11 March 2011
257481BV00003B/36/P